The Phoenix Living Poets

TIME ELSEWHERE

Poets Published in
The Phoenix Living Poets Series

★

JAMES AITCHISON
ALEXANDER BAIRD · ALAN BOLD
R. H. BOWDEN · FREDERICK BROADIE
GEORGE MACKAY BROWN
HAYDEN CARRUTH · JOHN COTTON
JENNIFER COUROUCLI
GLORIA EVANS DAVIES
PATRIC DICKINSON
TOM EARLEY · D. J. ENRIGHT
JOHN FULLER · DAVID GILL
PETER GRUFFYDD
J. C. HALL · MOLLY HOLDEN
JOHN HORDER · P. J. KAVANAGH
RICHARD KELL · LAURIE LEE
LAURENCE LERNER
CHRISTOPHER LEVENSON
EDWARD LOWBURY · NORMAN MACCAIG
ROY MCFADDEN
JAMES MERRILL · RUTH MILLER
LESLIE NORRIS · ROBERT PACK
ARNOLD RATTENBURY
ADRIENNE RICH · JON SILKIN
JON STALLWORTHY
GILLIAN STONEHAM
EDWARD STOREY · TERENCE TILLER
SYDNEY TREMAYNE
LOTTE ZURNDORFER

TIME ELSEWHERE

by

IRENE FEKETE

CHATTO AND WINDUS

THE HOGARTH PRESS

1971

Published by
Chatto & Windus Ltd
with The Hogarth Press Ltd
42 William IV Street
London W.C.2

*

Clarke, Irwin & Co Ltd
Toronto

ISBN O 7011 1791 5

Two of these poems, *Antiphon for Advent* and
The Last Siren first appeard in the *Cornhill*
Magazine

Distributed in the United States of America
by Wesleyan University Press

ISBN: O 8195 7035 4

Printed in Great Britain by
Lewis Reprints Limited
London and Tonbridge

Contents

For Osyth

A SCHOLAR WROTE

A scholar wrote (in Oxford,
City of the books, the bells,
Of the dead, old and new dead pressed
Against the stones, dead crowding
Narrow courts and walking on the grass)
In brittle cold he wrote
How a desert South of Sinai
Gave Elijah the cloak of fire,
How God (O crumpled don, O gentleman
With wit like the grin of Rameses)
In muddled omniscience troubled to mark
Cain's smooth forehead when no man lived
To regard the sign, no one at all,
Except his parents and himself.
A scholar wrote (in Oxford,
City of liturgies, Christ in quotations,
Quotations neatly turned from antique tongues)
Yet no one judged; thunderbolts did not come.

When finished, he walked to clear his mind—
Serene and undisturbed in twilight
He walked and cleared his mind of myths
(In Oxford, city of deliquescing towers,
City of the dead).

FROM AN OLD MAN'S DIARY

"... I had not arranged to live so long."

Gide

I had not arranged to live so long,
Too well polished glass pains my eyes,
Thin glass I am too weak to shatter;
All colours are grey
And my former hopes ought, like great age,
To lie damp in the ground,
Buried in black mould and quiet sleep.

To birds that come I fling some stones
I never had warm bread to give
Only stones smoothed perfect in my hand
Now so weakly thrown the birds do not depart:
Nothing sweet sings in my voiceless night.
All this I had not planned,
Like other old prophets, I had not foreseen.

CRUSADER'S TOMB

Sir Geoffrey, of this manor
Of this estate long held, whose name
Survives, whose begetting lives
—though elsewhere,
He lies in pious leisure, Cromwell's horse
Were not stabled here, his face
Is calm unmarred
His knee still bent, he went
To Jerusalem for the cross:
His knee is bent, he went
To Outremer, to blood, to crescent banners,
From the north country he rode
From the blue mists and all the rains,
The sweet uncomplaining quiet of the northern land;
He went out of love of God, a simple man.
Others before him, others wiser, better read,
They too had confused God with the sun.

REVENANT

Mr. Eliot, good evening
(In the public conveyance
The undignified vehicle
The mole, the segmented worm
The unmentionable object travailing
Within the entrails of honest London clay
We meet)
Good evening. Our eyes
Have met before
Some time ago
An imprecise age: I was young
And you were alive
Alive I assumed, probably, possibly
Alive or insufficiently moribund
To be earmarked for inurnment
Or set aside
For other particulat uses.
I recognize you now
By your sober bowler hat
(Like all the others in our plebian transport,
But of quality)
By your umbrella
(Indistinguishable from its fellows)
By the stoop of your shoulders
(You were always old and clerkly)
We exchange glances: I know you
Yet I do not cry out
This is a seemly encounter
I stare at your eyes, marvelling:
Still the eyes
Of the quintessential bird of the night
Day blind, peering
At the meticulous folds
Of a sixpenny paper.
Without dread I look into your eyes

10

Look past the spectacles
Past the faded iris
Past the immense pupils terribly dilated
And I recognize
Our mutual country:
Your knowledge is now more intimate,
I still batter at the guard rails
Rattle the logical skeleton
Of an ancient art.
Good evening.
(How cruel the silence of ghosts,
How uninformative)
You lower your eyelids,
Acknowledgement,
We have met before.

ISHTAR GATE

I would not advise Babylon:
Nothing to see, the merest trace
Of crumbling bricks, the wind's mouth there
Is stuffed with bitterness:
Without rhetoric are all its words.

But if you choose to go
Out of perversity, not love
(For in its dusts there are no loves,
Neither warriors nor women with black-rimmed eyes)
Read the signs, the shopworn moral and return
Quickly by the shortest road.

Above Babylon the clear night sky
Opens like a palm to read:
Few stars and no deceiving moon,
And there is her disaster—
Where the balance hangs, the twins embrace,
The archer hunts, on that narrow girdle of sky read:
Once the High Lady of the Moon
Searching for a lover went to hell
And found instead an unguessed truth:
She could not come forth again.

ATTICA

It sometimes rains in Attica,
The scattered posters do not remark
Upon the winter, the wind from Parnis
Or upon the mud of villages
Which have nothing to offer: where Plato did not teach,
Where there is no theatre for a festival,
Where even those lesser lights, the Byzantines,
Found nothing worth a fortress.

After all, it all is Athens,
The rest provides the view: plains, mountains,
The un-notable at night make their only contribution:
Small lights against a mountain's flank——a guide could say,
Remember where the Spartans made their camp.

BOEOTIA

They all are peasants.
They cannot refute the old abuse,
Not even in their proudest places
Where the grandest buildings stand
(Not temples but the blue and white
Institutes of Foreign Language.)

What can be done with them?
Cotton whitens the summer fields,
Their women have been taught to pick it;
They sit and loom the Parthenon
Into one thousand shoddy skirts.

The widows still wear black,
The widows and the poor
(In endless mourning for their poverty
They wear the livery of its ignorance)
And by the road old women squat
Swatting flies and cracking nuts
And the dust where they sit is a gate of Thebes.

LINES CONCERNING AN EPIPHANY

I am not certain what they saw
(Who will be duped by travellers' tales)
But I saw what gifts they took
And their faces when they returned:
The journey had not been as planned.

All these lands are rich in gods,
In virgin births and rising from the dead,
Wise men grow blind squinting at the stars:
But were they wise enough to read
And then to understand and act upon
An alien promise?

They took gold. That is proper for a king;
And myrrh: some scriptures mentioned death,
And frankincense—what one expects,
Perfectly acceptable to any god.
What then?
An ordinary child, his parents dumb with fear,
Gaping at the clothes, the crowns: peasants.
No sign in the faded stars.
Empty-handed our sages returned to us.

Now on their towers each rolls away
His precious scrolls, the small carved stones
Are locked in chests, the great windows
Open to the moon are closed
And through the cedar lattices the silver light
Makes cold white crosses on stone floors.

"It is finished," they say.
Doubtless the hardships of travel have marked their minds,
Perhaps the air of that far country is not safe,
Doubtless those people are overrich in prophecies
As we are in learned men to read them wrong.

"It is finished" and they often add "It is begun."
I find this impossible to understand.
The three old men live and come down from their towers
To walk among us on these winter nights
And they wear veils like women, thick and black,
But through heavy silk, unlined faces and golden beards
Shine like a summer sun.

1

The Window

High up she sat
Her hair not yellow but bright, the sun
Gifted it, the fire
Of afternoon burned and settled
On her head.
And in the window she turned and looked
Upon mountains
Only mountains were fit
For her to look upon.

Thus Queens sit, Queens in towers,
Queens Sovereign or in durance,
Queens who give judgment or without power
Give love and with idle fingers write
Our history.

2

The Gibbet

François they hung in winter
When chains are most cruel,
No verse saved him in the end, poor thief,
Only snow, foul snow to give him comfort
To hang upon his eyelids like a lover.
Strange the snow should be so kind to one so hot
He melted down
The frozen gargoyles with fires from his hell;
No mother ever wept for him.
Strange the snow should be so kind,
So gentle, noble to a thief:
So strange the snow, so kind.

17

The Last Trouvade

The old Queen is good for one last song
One last measure from Fontrevault
Not how she went to kiss the cross
But how she rode, an Amazon,
And how she outswore Royal France
And changed a monk for sovereign in her bed.
One last song for Queen Absolute
Of ten thousand poets
(She invented all our lies)
She, the Queen who dared judge love
(When we had sufficient of the precious stuff
To hazard it on a judgment)
One last song in the springtime of barren years
For an old Queen who peopled us with kings.

ANTIPHON FOR ADVENT

Sit in the sun
This last yellow light
Under the last leaves shrivelled on the vine:
The wine of the year is pressed,
Rejected on the stones are bitter grapes,
Dry, black and hard as winter earth; dead:
Sit in the sun

> *Rorate caeli desuper*——an age ago
> There was an island to the North
> Across its smoky seas men sailed:
> Brendan in a cockleshell
> Columba secure upon a cloak——
> Bringing news.
> Here be dragons: here be wonders——
> Martyred virgins walking to their graves
> Bearing their heads and gospel books:
> *Credo ut intellegam.*

Once in the sun
Lord Shiva danced, limbs of brass
Narrow feet of fire turning a wheel;
The Lord God danced, the sun big and hot
Burned on his ornaments and then a child,
A child unspoked the wheel: the Lord God
Of brass and fire
Turned to stone.

> *Veni Emmanuel:* some men have said
> God was fathered by a carpenter
> On a young maid newly wed or else
> Some said it was a commoner thing:
> A girl went to a spring in the afternoon,
> An ugly pitcher on her hip,
> And met a young man with a face of fire
> Then said she saw seraphim.
> *Ne timeas, Maria,*
> *Invenisti gratiam.*

19

The sun was dead
For a long winter in Pavia
But a philosopher made the best of it,
He wrote to save the little that he knew
Of the world that died about his feet
He wrote although he knew
Philosophy was no grey-eyed woman infinitely kind.
In time, inevitably, a distant king
Preferred him dead.

> *O Oriens, O Clavis David, O Sapientia*
> Love is no boy, blind and beautiful,
> Nor a woman wet with sea
> Love is a bone
> Hard and white as a holy rule,
> Difficult, the arcane law
> Established before the mountains—
> The cause of them.
> *Ostende nobis misericordiam tuam*
> And shall our bones flesh
> In a general resurrection?
> *Lux fulgebit super nos*
> Out of winter a child walks:
> No sun is dead.
> *Credo ut intellegam.*

PALLADIAN LAMENT

Come enriched by rain to a reflection of summer
Burning in dead wood,
Yellowing in ivory winter light,
Expiring: roses in pierced china jars
Exhale the incoherent spectre of perfume
Full of the futile breath of enclosed rooms;
The mathematics of window panes and fine proportion
Improve upon the disorders of other seasons
And the worm of age works with elegance of all things,
Leaving its mark to increase their value.
Here sit several virtues with naked breasts,
Grave and introspective upon their pediment
Having nothing to say to one another—
Deaf, blind, cold, dumb, immobile,
Gold leaf vines about their sandals
Suspended lustres before their eyes:
Restraint, on the order of antiquity,
Follows nicely all the lines in Pompey's hand,
Considers royal disaster carved in Caesar's skull
And re-engraved by Brutus on his thigh.
Containment is all:
Birth, death, love and passion in thick plaster
Wear shrouding dust till Judgement.
Only one uneasy question:
Did Bacchus and a Maenad unsuitably debauch?
Obviously not. Time is too silent and
Abandon too was frozen on a famous urn.

COUNTRIES

To take possession, explorer, plant no flag,
Put up no cross, no cairn
(A simple land could be so unwise,
Could mistake those symbols to mark a death
And not a birth)
But plant a tree and be secure
Plant a tree and for a hundred, hundred years,
When even marble has an end,
When marble is soft ochre dust
Suspended in the air, the tree will be a shelter
And the birds of half a world
May sit in it and sing
And singing,
Singing: the land is made beautiful.

There are no countries in the mind
Only landscapes in the heart,
The rocks, the skies incandescent
With the war of angels,
Rivers, placid, grey-green silent ooze
And suns, black with fire
Or anonymous, weak
Achieving few frail victories.
All lands are dust and bones,
Old charnels, neglected graves, sad places crowded
With shivering, naked, loveless ghosts
So everywhere you discover is the same,
The beasts unknown, the plants dark and full of poison.
For an exorcism
(No cairn, no holy water, no star, no cross:
Faith is a small candle melting a glacier
Melting sure but in a thousand thousand years and you
In one lifetime cannot wait so long)
For an exorcism plant a tree
And the birds will sit in it and sing.

From it the owl will hunt at night,
The small owl, golden eyed,
His feathered claws come to rest among its branches;
And by its roots the timid mouse,
The homeless mouse running grey beneath the moon
Shall shelter from the owl,
And in its roots, the dark sweet chambers of the earth
The other beasts, the small snuffling gentle beasts
Shall lie asleep, warm in winter
Dreaming of summer heats.
The birds sing,
Sing of dust and bones and the different lights of God
In a particular land
Made beautiful.

THE LAST SIREN

What more?
My throat gleams with oil,
I lift white arms to hail,
At my side
Against my thigh jewels are heaped,
A cloak is spread, wine is poured
Its fragrance marries with the wind which bells his sail.
My sisters, it is true, are dead;
Perhaps he is afraid of those thin bones upon the shore,
Imagines them the relics of my loves but I have never loved,
I have waited to behold one certain ship
Whose oars are red, whose painted sail
Proclaims its master wiser than Odysseus,
Odysseus who, after all, had little to commend him
Except the prowess of his lies.
What more?
I burn for the pale master of this ship which strays
So near the very tracery of surf.
If he passes? If he passes
Then I too shall go down to find my place
To rest among the ivory skulls, my sisters,
My sisters had a charm to lure their loves,
A rhyme they learned from Calliope:
I am not so fair as they, what more can I do
But reach out again? A long time ago
I forgot the song they used to sing.

CIRCA 363 A.D.

1. *The Apostate's Epitaph*

He did not deny the Sacraments
Or Charity and the one true Church
(Or other points saints choked upon
In the soured silence of their Thebaid tombs)
With any taint of cheap abuse
And certainly for no profit,
Unlike illustrious relatives
Who honoured Zeus or kissed a cross,
Whichever served to save their heads.

But rather,
Having gazed upon the sun too long
And being by nature too dearly fond
Of all old and elegant mistakes,
Having that refinement which cannot accept
So blasphemous a sacredness—
He nobly declined the proffered gift.

But war was the last book he read
And blood makes clear philosophy;
In ancient armour vulnerable to grace
He took his wound and changed his mind.

2. *In Memoriam*: *A Connoisseur*

The villa itself was fortified
Against any sort of Apocalypse,
Fat Titus had retired young,
The times were too disturbed
For political careers.
Instead he made a full collection
Of objects useful for his salvation
No matter which new creed was right.

He had: a marble Isis, an embalmed cat,
A reliquary of most odd design,
A blue lustre phial of Caesar's blood
And nine carnelian gnostic gems.
On a hazardous voyage to barbarous Thrace
He found a wooden goddess,
Rather vulgar, too well endowed,
But he bought her just the same:
He thought he might have need of her
When he passed a certain age.

And he bought important crosses,
Fashionable bits of splintered wood
Then two notable manuscripts:
A treatise handed down from Adam
And all the scriptures of the Jews.
He could afford three household priests
Of haughty competing sorts:
They passed each other on the stairs
With stiff uncharitable disdain.
And he read theology late at night
And keeping a bell close at hand
Could ring for baptism in his bed
Or a slaughter of heifers, were it required.
One afternoon he forgot a text
While unclasping the fine obsidian fish
Which held the folds of his reading robe
(Last moisture cloud or harm the stone)
Thus death and judgement found him all unarmed,
Quite naked, in his bath.

EX VOTO – ST. PANTELEMON

Honoured sir of the doubtful reputation,
In thick forests where the writ
Of more sceptical Councils does not run
You have candles, shrines, devotees
And confused clients who think your windlass
A sign of trade.
(Were you perhaps at sea?)
About you nothing can be fixed
Except you died, probably well, possibly at noon
In some hot, unkind place by some unusual means
Ingenious men devised
(Mankind is clever at tortures,
Far more inventive in pain than love)
Be that as it may:
I acknowledge I invoked
Nothing more than your uncertainty
But was not surprised to be well heard.

CLASSIC RELIEF

In cities not yet wholly new,
In unexpected quarters memory moves:
A blind man, black against the plastered walls,
Small, in the screaming heat of yellow light,
A blind man bent from his once-great height
Shuffles on the paving stones,
And his sad, brown-eyed younger daughter
Guides him by the hand:
All the streets are silent with respect
And the buildings which once were trees still hold
The nightingales he heard, that time before,
When first he came to die.

MEDITATION IN A ROMAN COFFEE BAR

Cor cordium. I do not understand dead languages
But I saw the rock and carving,
Something is beneath it
Grown from the embryo within
And after a term of pain, the difficult birth.
The subjects do not change,
Others sang and we re-mouth:
God, man, love
And the quick barque crossing Avernus:
Novelty is ornament poorly made,
An ancient craft debased:
But too well kept
Even great secrets die in silence:
We have become discretion incarnate
And wider passions flee in dismay
Before the academic caution of our love.
Cor cordium. Untranslated sacred rune,
Protect the ignorant from knowledge,
In pity, protect the wise
From the slow martyrdom of empty rooms.

DUMBARTON OAKS, A RECOLLECTION

After Shang bronzes, we took tea
Indoors, amid the orange trees,
Without the world was white,
Spring snow, beauty out of season.
Oblivious, we spoke of Ma Fei's brush,
Bronze mirrors, jade, rainbows of late T'ang glaze.
(But which right-minded mandarin
Would have chosen any one of us to be
Anything more than his witless concubine,
A second-best concubine in Shang H'ai silk?)

—and after tea, Byzantium
To come before El Greco and the wine;
We would take sherry in the late afternoon
With the light deep blue upon the Aubusson
Filtered through glass from colder blue without—
But before the wine, a library,
Patriarchs and Fathers of the Church,
Histories, eikons and shelves of cedar wood
A fragrance to mistake for incense.
I chose a book made for Holy Russia at her prayers,
An unknown liturgy.
I chose and opened and saints leapt up
A thousand flying virgins with their pointed feet,
Their arching feet beating golden air
Hovered above the formal rocks of paradise,
Above uncreated trees within the mind of God.
(But the hagiography is strict, too strict:
For a simile take flies in amber
Recall how long the empire was dead,
Dead and unburied in Byzantium:
Contrast in your memory an eikon's eye
With the glaring of a t'ao t'ieh
Or the gentle look of a Sung Kuan Yin).

But I chose
And the eye of God looked back at me,
I could not close the book.
(Confess your sin and be absolved, my child,
Confess, absolution hangs upon a word.
Which word, Father? Which, the first?
Confess, my child, and I will give you penance.
Father, are you wise enough to know
A Penance for so great a sin?
I saw God hard and naked as he is
And to merit absolution
Shall I describe his face?
Instead, an English compromise
Bless me Father, for I have sinned
Between tea and sherry at six o'clock
I lost my soul).

EIKON

They have taken from us the high language
Left us few words
And those words like Protestant divines
Stand mute
Dressed in dark clothes
Dark threadbare clothes
Hands clasped, hooded eyes gazing
Down.

We are the children of shopkeepers
And if there were princes in our line
They are forgotten:
The grit of time adheres
Even to the jars of cheap dutch gold
We reserve in cupboards
To gild our picture frames.

Frames.
Within and upon rectangles of wood
We preserve some images:
Not entirely aware
We nail epiphanies
To the walls of low ceilinged rooms
And we are not entirely lost.

They have taken from us the great pomps, the words,
The susurration of splendid stuffs
Falling to the tessellation of jewelled floors
But the mouth of the wind testifies
The sun is an imperial witness
And on our walls
The colours march
Their line unbroken
From genesis.

EDITORIAL BY A MUSE

When you have cleaned your fingernails,
Settled your viscera, adjusted to your glands,
Written your last rude words on lavatory walls,
Received a report with passing grades
At least in enunciation and courtesy, come back.
I may
If the temperature, the rapture of my disposition suits
me,
I may let you look on me again
But being a goddess and a Greek
I am naked and I observe my marble brightness
Has disarranged your souls.
Your enemies
(Oh yes, you have them,
They laugh at you behind their tea cups)
They tell me you have no souls;
How unkind the righteous are.
Go away, wash yourselves,
Mend up the pitiful shoddy you wear and come again
To let me look on you: I promise nothing,
I cannot restore wonder lost nor your own youth—
But I may teach you peace enough so you will walk
Silent and unnoticed, learning—
Or find reverence
At least in some other art.

TRIAD

1.

Yseult fasted.
In the proud tower Mark had built
And in the room he royally hung
With the woven pride of Byzantium
And the older nobility of Tyre,
She placed her hand upon a book
On a clean page where one small spell,
One short chain of names was set.

Tristan hunted.
He was away from her, in bog and mire
With sweating lords and swearing kerns,
In some danger from the sport
But he had no sport
For she had set a wound in him
(No greater, true, than one she bore
With patience, in herself).

And she thought,
Hand upon her book of spells
Where on other blacker pages
The gold beasts slept, the emerald birds
Devoured scarlet serpents and richer fruit,
The only thought he could not guess:
Would he have loved
Had he not drained the cup?

2.

Cassandra won her gift by fraud;
She cheated a divinity
With the imperious conceit
Of her sort of virtue

(A virtue not so rare
As elderly poets have supposed:
Not all the follies of the young are hot,
Many are follies cold as death).

And she won her tripod,
The fillet of white wool, the priestess' stave
(And the pity of young boys near the temple
Who could not understand
How a princess could weep
So often and so long).
She prophesied, cast certain spells
Which often did not charm
And had little enough to fill her time
Beyond envying Helen
(Not her beauty and not Paris
But the rich regard
Of wise men dreaming at the gates).

And in the end it was Agamemnon for a time;
He was ignoble but she was patient,
Standing in his chariot and knowing the end of it:
She even liked Clytemnestra when she saw
That regal bitch come from the palace
In flagrant garlands, treasonable jewels
And sumptuous, lying silk.
So with a kind of meek submission
(Which Apollo, seeing, envied as gods may envy)
Smiling, she went in to sacrifice.

3.

Elaine was middle-class or would have been
Had any cleric troubled to invent
A Latin label for her estate:
But in the forest there was nothing for comparison,

34

No Queens, no skilled magicians and her books
Were few, thin, cheaply bound in brown leather
For her father assumed that to be
A colour both modest and practical.

She could learn little;
The hag in the village knew the rhymes
For balsams, ointments and sick cows
And her maid was a little wiser
In the lore of moon-sets and binding threads.
It was not tragic but to be expected
That on the only afternoon which had some sun,
When the ancient mists dispersed
And her poor castle seemed almost tall,
That Lancelot should stop and she should love
Then die of it—not love but pure chagrin,
For all her spells were wrong.

ELEGIES

1.

The wind drops
The great tide
Pulled by the invisible moon
Oozes up the rimed beach:
See there, its probing fingers
Unlock the cliff,
The grass stiffens in the frost,
The first pebbles shift and fall:
Cliffs die.
        Have we buried them well, our dead?
        Sodden flowers in graveyards speak
        Of embarrassment,
        Of the inconvenience of mortality.
        Jericho has fallen,
        New customs do not condone
        The preservation
        Of heroic skulls beneath the hearth.
This is the eve of the day of the dead,
Here winter begins: a fact
Exactly like all others, exactly like
The black tide of blood
On which the barque of death
Moves without oars or wind
Toward us always
And never turns aside.

2.

Rising, the wind stirs,
Comes again, stretches the slack lines of air;
The warm breath of the shore
Hangs above cool waters, harmless,
The tide turns, the night becomes thin

Becomes a dark transparent skin
Lustrous and full of light: to be touched.
Between the pulse of silence
Discrete sounds of green evening
Reflect across clear water
And the tide runs.

I cannot remember winter.
I forget utterly, like God
When he is elsewhere occupied,
When he visits his famous Ethiopians:
I enjoy the new wind,
The Angelus of a secular bell,
A fragment of peace
And the conversation of eyes.

CONTINUOUS NARRATIVE

I open the winter box
Unfold the squares of wool and note
How in the darkness colours dimmed
How without use the cloth has thinned
Has lost its sheen
Has taken on the lines of age
Where in summer folds were made
Where fresh dried lavender was placed.
I open the box of winter and the room is full
Of the smell of passing time
Of sun sucking colour from these flowers
Leaving husks and the therapeutic fragrance
Of summers without incident.
Carefully cleaned wool and imprisoned dust:
The true smell of time gathering
Collecting in the dark
Where things out of sight grow old.

I walk out well clad,
Proof against the time of year:
How stately, how grave the passages of grey light,
How like a pallid godly man
The sky's face.
Suitably to secure employment
Runs the rectitude of streets
In good order stand permitted trees
Within their palings.
Their guards sweep from municipal grass
The last profusion of disorderly leaves
To feed their winter fires,
The winter fires without flame.
I go to my employment soberly:
In good time I will give my body to the fire
In good time I will merit
The burning of the leaves.

READINGS

Turn the page.
The book in the hand is
Hard, cold, the pages
Stir the air like children's ghosts;
The book in the hand
Peoples the empty house
Fills the empty glass
(And the colour of the wine is right,
Its pedigree attested by great men)
Turn the page,
The book in the empty house
Makes sound.

> Spake the Queen: I command a feast,
> Trumpets and the drum
> Spake the Knight: My sword.
> He drinks to her.

Curious how words shift and move,
This is an allegory, my mind
Plays the fine game with the pieces:
This is the soul, this is God, her love,
And these are the great tribulations,
The gates of Apocalypse.
Turn the page,
Read and breathe in
The particular smell of dead royalty,
Bound in red morocco.

> Spake the Queen: Thou alone, one.
> Spake the Knight: Thou incomparable.
> And they were lovers.

In a book what do words mean—
Were lovers—
Did breath come into it,
Or touch, or blood?

This book is so old, so long untouched,
Was it a word detached,
A title no one deserved?
Turn the page.
> Spake the Queen:
> Spake the Knight.
> Such courtesy is here
> That out of a spell and dark arts
> Comes absolution and entire joy.

All spells are embalmed in resin.
And through the amber white light seeps
Seeps down into the deep hidden parts
Which take on the colour of the sea floor:
Light breaks through the frail grey weeds,
So richly entombed here lie
The beautiful graves of dead false gods,
Turn.
> Rest in peace: the Queen's grave.
> Rest in peace: the ashes of her knight
> Above them the emerald arch
> Of winter's sky.

God of the dance of diagrams,
Of numbers added, multiplied, self-propagating,
The stars are littered with the consequence of Number
Ruminating upon Itself;
Calm, unchanging out to the rim of the universe
Where light and perhaps some love
Dies, is buried and is constantly reborn
In the resurrection of suns,
Turn the page.